THE MIND
OF A
LEADER

Developing Leadership Skills for the 21st Century

By

Floyd B. Pung

Copyright © {2022} Floyd B. Pung

THE MIND
OF A
LEADER

Developing Leadership Skills for the 21st Century

The Mind Of A Leader

"Leadership requires a wide range of abilities and characteristics, including communication, problem-solving, decision-making, and the ability to inspire and motivate people."

Table Of Contents

Introduction

Leadership is a skill that is vital in many sectors of life, including the job, civic groups, and even the household. Even in the home, leadership is essential. It requires the capacity to guide others in a certain direction, to excite and inspire those around you, and to create an environment in which individuals may collaborate effectively to achieve a common goal. The success of any business is directly related to the quality of the leadership that is provided inside that organization. Qualities necessary for effective leadership include integrity, vision, and communication. With the correct leadership, a team or organization may pursue its goals and objectives and reach new heights of accomplishment.

Leadership is a skill that is essential in many aspects of life, including the workplace as well as other settings. It involves the capacity to define direction, encourage and inspire others, and foster an environment in which people can work together to accomplish success. Integrity, vision, and communication are just a few of the qualities that make up effective leadership, and they are all vital to the success of any business in terms of accomplishing its goals and objectives. Teams and organizations have the potential to flourish and achieve new heights if they are led effectively.

....

Charles was a natural-born leader. He was the one who always made sure that everyone was on target, but he also made sure that everyone felt appreciated by paying attention to people's feelings and making sure that everyone felt important. He was a fantastic listener, and people always felt comfortable coming to him with their concerns.

At work, Charles was always the one that everyone else came to for guidance. He was able to think strategically and was consistently one step ahead of his contemporaries at all times. He was able to make difficult choices and motivate his team to persevere through even the most challenging of tasks because of his leadership.

Outside of the workplace, Charles was a driven and passionate leader. He was interested in his local community, volunteered in his church, and was a mentor to many young people in his neighborhood. He had a firm conviction that everyone should be given the chance to realize their full potential and was constantly looking for new ways to have a positive influence on the world.

In every meaning of the word, Charles exemplified what it means to be a true leader.

He had the ability to inspire and motivate those around him, and he was constantly looking for new ways to make a difference in the world. He was an example of what great leadership looks like and will always be recognized as such. Describe the difficulties that Charles encountered in his role as a leader.

As a leader, Charles had to overcome a lot of obstacles. He frequently had to make challenging choices that demanded a significant amount of careful thought and deliberation on his part. In addition to this, he had to figure out how to communicate clearly with the members of his team and make sure that everyone was on the same page. He had to educate himself on how to excite and drive his team while also maintaining respect for them and an awareness of their requirements.

In addition to this, Charles needed to learn how to cope when he was unsuccessful. He was ultimately accountable for the success or failure of his team, and as a leader, he needed to learn how to deal with the disappointment of failure and move on with his life.

In the end, Charles needed to figure out how to satisfy both his own requirements and those of his team.

Even though he had to make sure that his team was successful, he also had to make sure that he had time to recover and get his energy back up. This was very essential to him.

As a leader, Charles had to deal with a lot of difficult situations, but he was always up for the challenge. He had a strong commitment to leadership and was constantly on the lookout for new ways that he and his team might better. He served as a model for what it means to be a great leader, and for that reason, he will be remembered forever in that capacity.

In order to resolve the issues, he was having with his leadership, Charles took a number of concrete actions. First, he honed his abilities to communicate effectively and listen attentively. He made it a point to hear everyone's perspectives and concerns, and he was able to articulate his own thoughts and objectives in a clear and convincing manner.

In addition to that, he concentrated on fostering relationships with the people on his team. He exerted a lot of effort to gain everyone's confidence and cultivate a setting in which they could freely share their thoughts and opinions.

Charles sought to foster an environment that values teamwork and creativity. He inspired his staff to think creatively and adventurously, as well as to take risks, and he made sure they had the resources and support they required to do so successfully.

In the end, Charles focused his efforts on improving his own leadership abilities. He educated himself on the topic of effective leadership by studying various texts, including books, attending seminars, and going to school. He was constantly on the lookout for new ways that he and his team could get better. Charles took a variety of actionable initiatives, and in the end, his enthusiasm and commitment paid off. He served as a model for what it means to be a great leader, and for that reason, he will be remembered forever in that capacity.

CHAPTER1

Comprehending What Leadership Is

Taking charge, inspiring, and directing others toward the accomplishment of a shared objective are all essential components of effective leadership. It is a valuable trait that contributes to an individual's success in life and in the positions that they play. Leaders are frequently the ones that have to make challenging decisions, provide others with direction and assistance, and inspire people to perform to the best of their abilities.

Leadership requires a wide range of abilities and characteristics, including communication, problem-solving, decision-making, and the ability to inspire and motivate people. Leaders who are effective are able to inspire and motivate their teams to accomplish what they set out to do. They are aware of the requirements that must be met by their team and are able to provide direction and oversight. In addition to this, they are capable of staying organized and delegating chores and responsibilities.

It is essential for leaders to have a distinct mental picture of the end result they are working toward. They should be able to convey that vision to their team and supply them with the resources and support they need to be successful in achieving that vision. The ability to adjust one's course of action in response to shifting circumstances and remain flexible is another essential quality for leaders to possess.

The ability to encourage one's team is another essential quality for a leader to possess. This requires an awareness of the capabilities and limitations of one's team, as well as the ability to supply members with the necessary support and resources. In addition to being able to acknowledge and reward triumphs, leaders should also be able to deliver constructive criticism when it is required.

In the end, gaining an understanding of leadership means having a firm grasp of the personal qualities and practical abilities that are essential to effective leadership. Leaders are expected to have strong communication skills, the ability to motivate their team, the ability to delegate duties, and the ability to maintain organization. In addition to this, they need to have a distinct idea of the objective they are working for and the capacity to adjust when circumstances shift.

Effective leaders possess these characteristics, which enable them to inspire and encourage their teams to accomplish their objectives.

A. Definition of a leader?

The ability to encourage, inspire, and direct a group of individuals toward a single objective is an essential component of leadership. Developing a vision for the future, coming up with methods to realize that goal, and putting together teams to put those plans into action are all required steps. In addition to that, it involves the ability to communicate clearly, cultivate meaningful connections, and make sound judgments.

The ability to advise, motivate, and enable individuals and teams to work toward common objectives is an essential component of leadership. Creating a goal that everyone can get behind, coming up with plans to achieve that vision, and putting together a group of people who are willing and able to collaborate effectively in order to put those plans into action are all required steps. To be a good leader, you need to be able to communicate effectively, cultivate connections, and make decisions that are in line with the values and goals that everyone shares.

In addition to this, leadership requires accepting responsibility for the activities and results achieved by the team while also motivating others to follow suit.

B. Traits a Good Leader Should Possess

1. A crystal clear vision of the future for the group is something that all good leaders possess. They share this goal with the members of the team, and they motivate those people to strive toward realizing the vision.

2. Communication: Leaders are able to successfully convey both their vision and their strategy to the members of their team. They also pay attention to the input provided by the team and make improvements as required.

3. Capacity for Swift and Unwavering Decision-Making Leaders are able to make decisions swiftly and unwaveringly. They are aware of the outcomes that can be expected from each choice, and they are willing to accept responsibility for them.

4. Establishing Relationships: In order to establish respect and trust among members of the team, leaders must first establish relationships with those individuals. In addition to this, they foster an atmosphere of cooperation and support for one another.

5. Inspiring Others to Work Hard and Do Their Best
Leaders are able to motivate and inspire the members of their team to job hard and do their best work. They cultivate an environment that is full of excitement and determination to realize the common goal. Create more characteristics of leadership through writing.

6. Motivation: A leader is someone who knows how to motivate their team, how to recognize and reward good work and development, and how to motivate themselves. They are able to recognize any problems that are preventing progress and devise solutions for such problems.

7. Accepting responsibility: Leaders are aware that they are ultimately responsible for the triumphs and failures of their teams. They lead by example by accepting responsibility for the deeds and choices made by their team and encouraging others to do the same.

8. Adaptability: The ability to modify one's approach and methods in response to changing circumstances is essential for leaders. They are aware of the significance of being adaptable and flexible in response to the various challenges they face.

9. Empowerment Leaders are aware of the significance of providing their teams with the authority to make decisions and the responsibility to own the work that they do.

10. Resolving Conflict: A key characteristic of effective leaders is the ability to recognize and constructively manage disagreements that arise among members of a team. They are aware of the significance of finding solutions to problems in a timely and efficient manner.

11. Integrity: All of a leader's dealings are conducted in an honest and ethical manner, and they have a strong sense of personal integrity. They are exemplary people who aim to lead by setting a positive example for others.

12. Resilience: Leaders are able to maintain their path of action in spite of obstacles and failures because they have the fortitude and bravery to do so. They are able to maintain their composure and resiliency in spite of the challenges they are facing.

13. Delegation: Leaders are aware of the significance of delegating responsibilities to the members of their teams in order to make the best possible use of the resources available to them.

14. Empathy is the ability to put oneself in the position of another person in order to better understand their difficulties and requirements. Leaders possess this ability. They are able to provide assistance and direction whenever it is required.

15. A great grasp of one's own strengths and flaws, as well as the ability to use this information to one's advantage Leaders have a strong understanding of both their own strengths and weaknesses. They are also capable of recognizing the shifting requirements of their team and adapting to those needs.

B. The Advantages of Taking on a Leadership Role

Leadership is a priceless skill that can be applied to both one's personal life and one's professional life for positive results. Leadership can be defined as the capacity to exert influence over other people and to inspire them to work toward a shared objective. To ensure the continued success of an organization, strong leadership is an absolute requirement. The following are some of the advantages of holding a leadership position:

1. An improvement in the overall performance of the team: A successful leader will be able to bring out the best in each member of the team, thereby assisting those members in cooperating toward the accomplishment of a common objective. The improved performance of the team as a whole will, in the end, lead to increased levels of production and efficiency.

2. Increased Engagement and Motivation A strong leader will be able to provide the members of the team with direction and guidance, which will result in increased engagement and motivation. This results in improved morale and loyalty among employees, as well as an overall improvement in the quality of the working environment.

3. Improved Communication A strong leader will be able to communicate effectively with the other members of the team, making sure that everyone is on the same page in terms of the goals and objectives, and that they all have the same understanding of them. The enhanced communication will contribute to the formation of a team that is more cohesive and productive.

4. Enhanced Capacity to Solve Problems: Leaders are adept at spotting issues and finding solutions to them in a timely and effective manner. Because of this, teams are better able to work through difficult problems in a timely manner, which contributes to an overall improvement in their problem-solving ability.

5. Enhanced Creativity Effective leaders are able to create an atmosphere that is conducive to creativity and innovation. In this environment, individuals on the team are encouraged to think creatively and come up with new concepts. This has the potential to lead to significant advances and streamlined procedures.

Leadership is an important talent that can have a good impact not just on individuals but also on the companies in which they are employed. It may be extremely useful to take the time to build and enhance your leadership skills. Ultimately, this will result in higher team performance, increased engagement, improved communication, improved problem-solving and increased creative output.

CHAPTER 2.

Acquiring Effective Leadership Abilities

Developing abilities in leadership might be difficult, but it is possible to accomplish so with the right amount of effort and attention. The ability to encourage, inspire, and instruct others is a necessary component of leadership qualities. In addition to these, there are things like communicating, making decisions, finding solutions to problems, and cultivating a pleasant environment.

The first thing you need to do in order to build your leadership skills is to pinpoint the specific areas in which you feel you could use some improvement. Consider the aspects of your performance that need improvement the most, and center your efforts there. Once you have determined the aspects of your game that require improvement, the next step is to think of strategies to improve them. This may involve engaging in activities such as taking classes, going to seminars, or reading books on the subject of leadership.

It is essential that you put the new abilities you are acquiring into practice. This may involve coordinating a project or guiding a group of people in its completion.

You might try to take on more responsibility in your current work, such as leading meetings or delegating chores. This is another option open to you.

It is also very important to pay attention to the perspectives of other people and to be receptive to their comments. You should be willing to grow as a result of your failures and adapt your strategy appropriately.

In conclusion, it is essential to keep a positive mindset and remain motivated throughout the process. This will assist you in maintaining your concentration on your goals and will motivate those around you.

It takes time and works to develop abilities in leadership, but it is possible to accomplish so through devotion and consistent practice. You have the potential to develop into a successful leader if you have the correct mindset and access to the resources.

1. Determine Which Areas Need Improvement The first thing you should do while working on strengthening your leadership skills is to determine which areas need improvement. Consider the aspects of your performance that need improvement the most, and center your efforts there.

2. Increase Your Knowledge Once you have determined the aspects of your performance that require improvement, the next step is to determine how you might improve them. This may involve engaging in activities such as taking classes, going to seminars, or reading books on the subject of leadership.

3. Putting what you've learned into practice is another crucial step in the process of acquiring new skills. This may involve coordinating a project or guiding a group of people in its completion. You might try to take on more responsibility in your current work, such as leading meetings or delegating chores. This is another option open to you.

4. Pay Attention to Other People It is also very important to pay attention to the viewpoints of other people and to be receptive to feedback. You should be willing to grow as a result of your failures and adapt your strategy appropriately.

5. Retain Your Motivation As a final point of emphasis, it is necessary to keep a positive attitude and to retain your motivation. This will assist you in maintaining your concentration on your goals and will motivate those around you.

A. Figuring Out What Your Strong Points Are

Finding out what components of your personality and skill set are most advantageous to you in reaching success can be an extremely helpful exercise, and one of those aspects is figuring out what your strengths are. Reflecting on one's prior experiences, participating in personality assessments, or inquiring about the viewpoints of one's friends and family members are all good ways to discover one's talents. Some people have difficulty recognizing their own capabilities in this regard.

When you are contemplating the events of the past, give some thought to the pursuits or responsibilities that you have found to be the most satisfying and fruitful. Think about the things you do that you find to be the most enjoyable and satisfying, and try to figure out why this is the case. This might assist you in determining which of your inherent strengths are most prominent.

Personality tests can also be helpful in assisting with the identification of an individual's strengths. These examinations can be completed in person or online and typically include questions concerning the way in which you respond to a variety of responsibilities and scenarios.

The results of these tests can help you get insight into the many domains in which you thrive.

Last but not least, it may be beneficial to solicit the opinions of those who are closest to you. Ask your close friends and family members what they believe your inherent abilities are, and make sure to take their input into consideration. They might be able to point out areas of strength that you haven't recognized yourself but could help you improve in those areas.

Discovering what aspects of your personality and background give you a distinct advantage over other people can be a fruitful activity that can help you understand what sets you apart from others and direct your attention to the domains in which you are most likely to be successful. Spending some time figuring out what you do well may be an energizing and successful experience that can lead to increased levels of self-confidence and accomplishment.

B. Increasing One's Own Self-Awareness

Having the capacity to notice and comprehend one's own feelings, behaviors, and thoughts is an essential step in the process of developing self-awareness. In order to effect positive changes in one's life, it is essential to possess this skill.

The ability to understand our own strengths, shortcomings, and motives is a key component of self-awareness. It also helps us develop stronger connections, improve our decision-making, and accomplish our goals more effectively.

Discovering the aspects of your life that may use some work is an essential stage in the process of cultivating self-awareness, and it is also one of the most significant steps. This can involve analyzing your past acts and thinking about how those choices have influenced your life in the present and the future. It may also require analyzing your current patterns of behavior and deciding what sorts of adjustments are necessary.

It is imperative that you take action once you have determined the areas in which there is room for development. This could entail activities such as goal-setting, the execution of plans, and the monitoring of progress. In addition, it could be useful to ask for feedback from other people so that you can obtain an understanding of how your behavior is perceived by others.

It is essential to engage in self-care practices in addition to carrying out the necessary actions. This entails taking care of your mental, emotional, and physical health all at the same time. This could involve getting the recommended amount of sleep, maintaining a healthy diet, and participating in pursuits that bring you pleasure.

Last but not least, it is essential to maintain awareness of both your internal ideas and feelings. You can develop a deeper comprehension of yourself and your responses to various circumstances if you take the time to name and acknowledge the feelings that you experience and allow yourself to feel them.

Increasing one's level of self-awareness is a process that continues throughout one's life and requires both time and effort. Nevertheless, it is an essential move that has the potential to improve your life in a number of ways. You may identify areas in which you could improve, take measures to make good changes, and engage in self-care if you have a healthy dose of self-awareness.

C. Having an Awareness of Your Surroundings

It is absolutely necessary, in order to live a successful and meaningful life, to have an understanding of the context in which you find yourself.

The environment is comprised of our physical, spiritual, and social circumstances, all of which have an effect on and contribute to the formation of our life. It encompasses not just our homes and places of employment but also our communities and the entire world.

It is essential to have a good understanding of and appreciation for your surroundings by gaining knowledge about the natural and man-made components that make up your environment. If we have a better understanding of the environment, we will be better equipped to make judgments about how to engage with the world around us and how to coexist with the natural world.

Learning about the geography, history, and culture of your surroundings is an important part of environmental awareness. It is possible for us to better comprehend how to engage with the natural environment if we are familiar with the local flora, fauna, and climate. When we have an understanding of the history and culture of a region, we can gain a better understanding of how the actions we take now will affect the future.

Personal experience can also serve as a valuable resource for environmental education. A better comprehension of the world that surrounds us can be attained through activities such as observation and engagement with the natural world. We also have the opportunity to cultivate relationships with members of our communities, which can result in the acquisition of fresh insights and a deeper respect for the natural world.

To live a life that has significance, it is essential to have a good understanding of the world around you. It has the potential to assist us in making decisions that are more well-informed and to provide us with a deeper comprehension of our place in the world. If you are unable to comprehend your surrounding area, you will have a greater propensity to make terrible decisions and to lead a life that is unconnected and devoid of satisfaction.

D. Putting Together Your Group

As a leader, one of your most critical and challenging responsibilities is to build a strong team. It calls for thoughtful consideration, cautious planning, and methodical action.

Because the members of your team that you choose to work with will form the basis of your success as a leader, it is essential to choose the appropriate individuals for your team.

The first thing you should do is figure out what kind of team you require. Take into consideration the tasks that need to be finished, as well as the abilities, experiences, and backgrounds that might be helpful in finishing those tasks. The next step is to compose a job description for the group, detailing the required responsibilities and abilities.

After you have the job description in hand, it is time to begin searching for and recruiting qualified candidates for the position. Post job openings on online job boards, conduct searches for and make contact with prospective applicants, and network to develop relationships with people who might one day join your company. To decide who the greatest potential team members are, conduct interviews and use other types of assessment techniques.

After you have chosen the members of the team, it is essential to orient and onboard them in the appropriate manner. The team's mission, goals, and expectations should all be communicated, and any appropriate training and resources should be made available.

After the team has been assembled, it is essential to maintain communication with each member and continue to offer guidance and support. To ensure that the team is moving in the right direction, it is important to define their objectives and hold regular meetings to monitor their progress. Commemorate your victories, and find speedy and just solutions to any problems that arise.

As a leader, one of your primary responsibilities is to build a team, which is a challenging but ultimately rewarding endeavor. The cornerstone of your success as a leader will be the team that you establish, and the success of that team will be the success of you as a leader. You need to grow your team up to the level of quality that you require, and you need to take care of them so that they may achieve continuing success. It may be extremely detrimental to both your business and your leadership if you are unable to construct the appropriate team or give them the necessary support and resources to do their jobs.

E. Engaging in Constructive Communication

Effective communication is essential to one's success in the role of a leader. To make sure that everyone is on the same page and working together to reach a common objective, it is necessary to have the capacity to communicate in a way that is clear, succinct, and organized.

To get things started, it is essential to have an active listening posture. This requires not only listening to what is being said but also comprehending the meaning of what is being said and acting accordingly. Take the time to check in with everyone and make sure that they are comprehending what is being said by asking questions.

The ability to articulate one's ideas and thoughts in a way that is both crystal clear and succinct is another crucial aspect of effective communication. This involves eliminating jargon and utilizing language that is simple and easy to grasp. In addition, if you want the support of your team, it is essential to be able to articulate the thought process that went into making the judgments you did.

In addition to this, it is essential to have the ability to identify and resolve any misconceptions or disagreements that may come up.

It is crucial to have the capacity to remain cool and neutral while also having the ability to be assertive. This will contribute to the creation of a positive atmosphere and will encourage teamwork.

Last but not least, it is essential to have the capacity to offer feedback in a manner that is constructive. Be sure to provide instances of positive reinforcement when they are called for, and give clear examples of what aspects of their performance could want improvement.

It is absolutely necessary to have efficient communication in order to guarantee that everyone is on the same page and working towards the same objective. A leader may secure the success of their team and keep their members motivated by acquiring the necessary communication skills. As a leader, it is important to be receptive to different viewpoints and constructive criticism, to be willing to listen, and to be able to communicate clearly.

CHAPTER 3

Implementing Leadership in Everyday Situations

Leadership is a skill that is crucial to have in any workplace, regardless of the size of the company you work for. This includes both small businesses and major corporations. Learning how to lead effectively involves commitment and practice, and in order to be an effective leader, one must be willing to put leadership into practice throughout the course of their own time.

Creating an unmistakable picture of what lies ahead is the initial step in putting one's leadership skills into action. A leader is someone who is able to recognize what the organization requires and figure out how to provide for those requirements in the most effective manner. To accomplish this, you will need to have an in-depth knowledge of the organization as well as the capacity to think strategically about its objectives. It is essential to keep one's eye on the bigger picture in order to ensure the continued health and prosperity of the firm.

Creating a strategy is the second step that needs to be taken. Specifically, this entails the formulation of goals and objectives, as well as methods for their accomplishment. A leader is someone who can convey the plan of action to the team, make sure that everyone knows the plan, and ensure that everyone is committed to the strategy. Leaders that are effective will also be able to assign duties in an efficient manner, in addition, to providing direction and assistance to ensure that their objectives are reached.

The strategy must next be put into action, which is the third step. A leader is someone who can take action and is willing to accept responsibility for the outcomes of the choices they make. This includes keeping track of progress, providing comments, and modifying plans as required. Additionally, leaders need to be willing to take chances and adapt whenever it is required to do so.

The conclusion of this process is the fourth stage, which entails analyzing the outcomes of the plan and modifying it as required. A leader needs to be able to analyze the success of their plans in an impartial manner and make any required adjustments to those plans. It is essential for a leader to have the ability to incorporate the comments and suggestions made by their team into ongoing improvement efforts.

A leader can ensure that their organization is successful and can continue to grow and thrive if they put leadership into practice and ensure that their organization is successful. Leadership is a necessary skill, and being a successful leader requires a commitment to the cause as well as plenty of practice.

A. Establishing Objectives

The establishment of objectives is a fundamental component of effective leadership. Leaders are able to provide their teams and the organization as a whole with a road map to success by setting goals that are SMART, which stands for specified, measurable, attainable, realistic, and timely.

It is the responsibility of leaders to ensure that goals are consistent with the organization's mission and values. Goals ought to be ambitious but not insurmountable, and they should be revised whenever necessary. Leaders are also responsible for providing their teams with the resources and assistance they need to achieve their goals.

In addition to deciding what they want to accomplish, leaders must devise strategies for how they might do it.

This plan ought to include distinct actions, as well as dates so that the team is aware of what should be done and when it should be done. It is also the leader's responsibility to convey the team's goals and plan. Because of this, it is easier for everyone to maintain their motivation and stay on the same page.

Additionally, leaders are responsible for monitoring the success of their teams and providing feedback to those teams. This enables the team to monitor their progress and make any required adjustments as the situation warrants. The leaders of the team should also be receptive to the feedback of their members and change the strategy accordingly.

Lastly, leaders have an obligation to acknowledge and commend the accomplishments of their teams. This encourages positive conduct and contributes to the team's motivation to continue working toward their goal of success.

The process of goal-setting is a crucial component of effective leadership. Leaders may map out a path to victory for their teams and organizations by paying attention to the advice presented above and following it.

B. The Process of Making Decisions

One of the most significant parts of being successful is the ability to make judgments in a leadership role. Your role as a leader requires you to make decisions that are in the best interest of the organization as a whole and the various people who have a stake in it. This can be a challenging endeavor because there are frequently a variety of views to take into account and competing interests to evaluate.

Gathering up as much information as you can is the first thing you need to do in order to make the right choice. This includes conducting research on the subject, talking with specialists and stakeholders, and obtaining an opinion from individuals whose lives may be changed as a result of the decision. After you have gathered enough information, it is essential to think about all of the possibilities and assess them in an unbiased manner. It is also crucial to analyze how the choice will affect the future of the organization and to weigh the potential downsides and upsides of each alternative.

When it comes to selecting a choice, it is essential to make use of your talents in critical thinking and to ensure that you are acting in a logical and rational manner.

You should also make it a goal to have an open mind and be willing to think about things from other points of view. In conclusion, it is critical to exhibit decisiveness and act with self-assurance. This will reveal to others that you are a capable and effective leader while also helping to motivate them.

Making decisions as a leader can be challenging, but if you approach the task with the appropriate mentality and approach, it is possible to achieve success. You'll be able to make the greatest decisions for your business and the people who have a stake in it if you start by obtaining all of the relevant information, considering all of the potential courses of action, weighing the costs and benefits, and acting decisively.

C. Delegating Tasks

As a leader, one of the most important things you can do is delegate responsibilities to other people. It requires communicating to members of the team that they will be held accountable for the tasks and duties they are given and then allocating those tasks and obligations to them. Leaders are able to concentrate on the wider picture and guarantee that their teams are making progress toward the overarching goals of the organization when they delegate duties to their subordinates.

It is crucial to be precise and concise about what you anticipate from each individual member of the team when you are allocating work. Provide a comprehensive explanation of the assignment, together with any relevant expectations and due dates. In addition to this, it is essential to offer assistance and direction throughout the entire process. This includes actively listening to criticism and making oneself available to answer questions or resolve any concerns that may come up.

When allocating responsibilities, it is essential to take into account the skills and qualifications of every member of the team.

This helps to ensure that the most qualified individual is given the assignment and that the individual has the requisite skills and expertise to successfully accomplish the task.

In conclusion, it is essential to acknowledge and appreciate excellent work. It can be helpful to drive members of a team to continue exceeding expectations and achieving their objectives if they are recognized for completing duties to an exceptionally high standard.

It is impossible to be an effective leader without the ability to delegate work. It enables leaders to concentrate on the wider picture and makes it possible for them to monitor whether or not their teams are making progress toward their objectives. It has the potential to lead to a more successful and productive team if it is carried out effectively.

D. Finding Solutions to Conflicts

When it comes to finding a solution to a problem, effective leadership is a crucial component. In order to effectively settle disagreements, leaders need to think strategically and apply their communication and problem-solving skills. The first thing that has to be done in order to resolve a conflict is to pinpoint the underlying concerns.

Before attempting to find a solution to the disagreement, those in positions of authority need to compile all of the pertinent data and points of view. This will be of assistance to leaders in determining the underlying cause of the conflict and developing an efficient approach for its resolution.

After the underlying problem has been recognized, those in positions of authority should cooperate to devise a solution that is beneficial to all parties involved. In this, the requirements, wants, and interests of each party should be taken into consideration. Every individual who has a stake in the matter should be given the opportunity to express their thoughts and concerns, and those in positions of authority should make it a point to listen attentively to do so.

In addition to this, leaders should establish a schedule and establish clear expectations for the resolution. This will serve to instill a feeling of urgency as well as accountability, which will, in turn, contribute to the resolution process remaining on its intended path. In addition, leaders should be ready to provide direction and assistance whenever it is required to help guarantee that the process of conflict resolution is successful.

Last but not least, the leaders in charge need to make sure that everyone involved is content with the resolution. Because of this, it will be far less likely that the conflict will flare up again in the future. In order for leaders to be successful in preventing future confrontations, they should make it a priority to keep lines of communication open and cultivate an environment that values respect and collaboration.

Leaders may effectively resolve issues and establish an environment of trust and mutual respect by following these steps and working through the process.

Summary

This book, The Mind of a Leader: Developing Leadership Skills for the 21st Century, provides a complete review of the process of leadership, beginning with an understanding of the basics of leadership and ending with the implementation of those skills. It starts off by examining what leadership is and the characteristics that make a good leader, and then it moves on to teaching the skills that are required to be successful. After that, it discusses how to put such abilities into practice, including how to set goals, make decisions, delegate responsibilities, and resolve disagreements. In the end, it comes to a close with a brief review of the most important takeaways. The readers of this book will gain the information and tools necessary to become effective leaders in the 21st century as a result of reading this book.